THE COLORING ARTIST
OF THIS BOOK IS:

_____

ÍCARO

EDITORES

Ícaro Editores
www.icaroeditores.com

© 2016 Arturo Garcia
www.arturogarciafineart.com
arturogarciafineart@gmail.com

ISBN-13: 978-1539170150
ISBN-10: 1539170152

Cover Design: Ícaro Editores
Interior Design: Ícaro Editores

Animal World

A MAGICAL AND INTERACTIVE COLORING JOURNEY THROUGH THE WORKS OF ARTURO GARCIA

Adult *and* *Kids* Coloring Book
ARTURO GARCIA

This coloring book is the product of the last four years of painting nonstop and includes all my animal collections: Africa, Colorado Wildlife, Marine Wildlife, Yellowstone, Animal Farm and Life!

The imperfections on the images are not deliberate, they are the result of the process, which was 100% by hand, meaning that a computer wasn´t used to create the images. The entire book is an artisan compilation of my own oil paintings.

At first it kind of bothered me that some lines went beyond their course while others didn´t quite get there. But then I surrendered to the conclusion that imperfection has a charisma of its own; it means, in a way, that the human hand was there and not a machine.

About the pattern: I wanted to come as close as possible to the pattern of my original paintings to give everyone the opportunity to re-create my work by interacting with the original paintings using all coloring tools available such as color pencils, markers, crayons or inks. The suggested instruction is simple: go to www.arturogarciafineart.com click on the painting you are about to color and go from there!

I hope you experience the relaxation I experience when I paint. I hope you share this book with those you love, and more than anything, I hope you have lots of fun coloring.

Arturo Garcia.-

Este libro de colorear es el producto de los últimos cuatro años de pintar sin parar, e incluye todas mis colecciones de animales: África, Animales Salvajes de Colorado, Animales Marinos, Granja de Animales, y Vida!

Las imperfecciones en las imágenes no son a propósito, sino el resultado del proceso que fue 100% a mano, es decir no se utilizó la computadora para crearlas. El libro entero es una compilación artesanal de mis propias pinturas al óleo.

Al principio me quiso molestar que algunas líneas se pasaban de la raya mientras que otras no llegaban. Pero luego me rendí a la conclusión de que la imperfección tiene su propio carisma; significa, en cierta forma, que la mano humana estuvo allú y no una máquina.

Acerca del estampado: Quise acercarme lo más posible al estampado o patrón de trazo de aquél de mis óleos originales para darles la oportunidad de recrear mi trabajo al interactuar con las pinturas originales utilizando todos los materiales de colorear disponibles como lápices de colores, marcadores, crayones o tintas. La instrucción sugerida es simple: visitar mi sitio web www.arturogarciafineart.com, dar click a la pintura que se va a colorear ¡y partir de allí!

Espero que experimenten la relajación que yo experimento cuando pinto. Espero que compartan este libro con sus seres queridos, y más que todo, ¡deseo que se diviertan mucho coloreando!

Arturo García.-

Africa

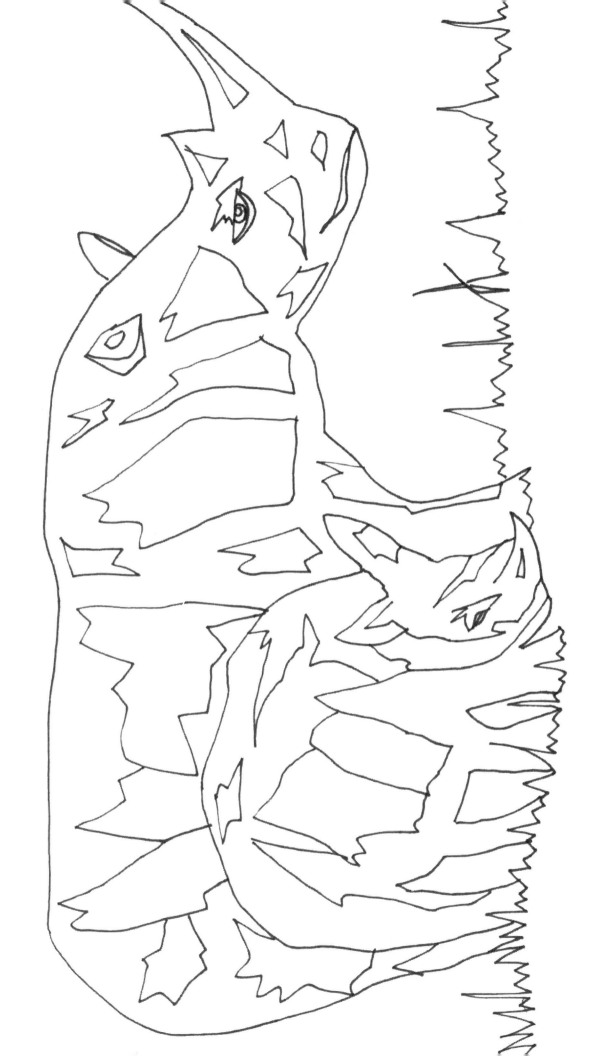

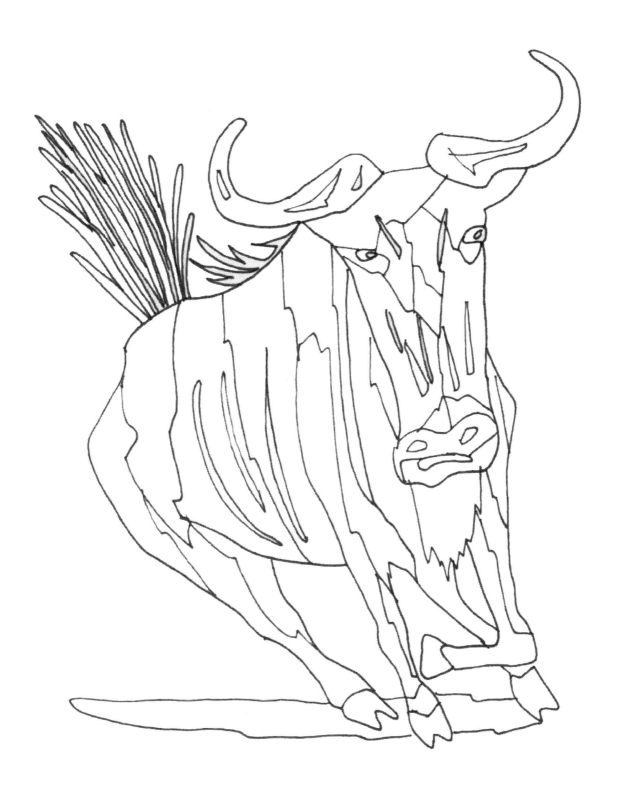

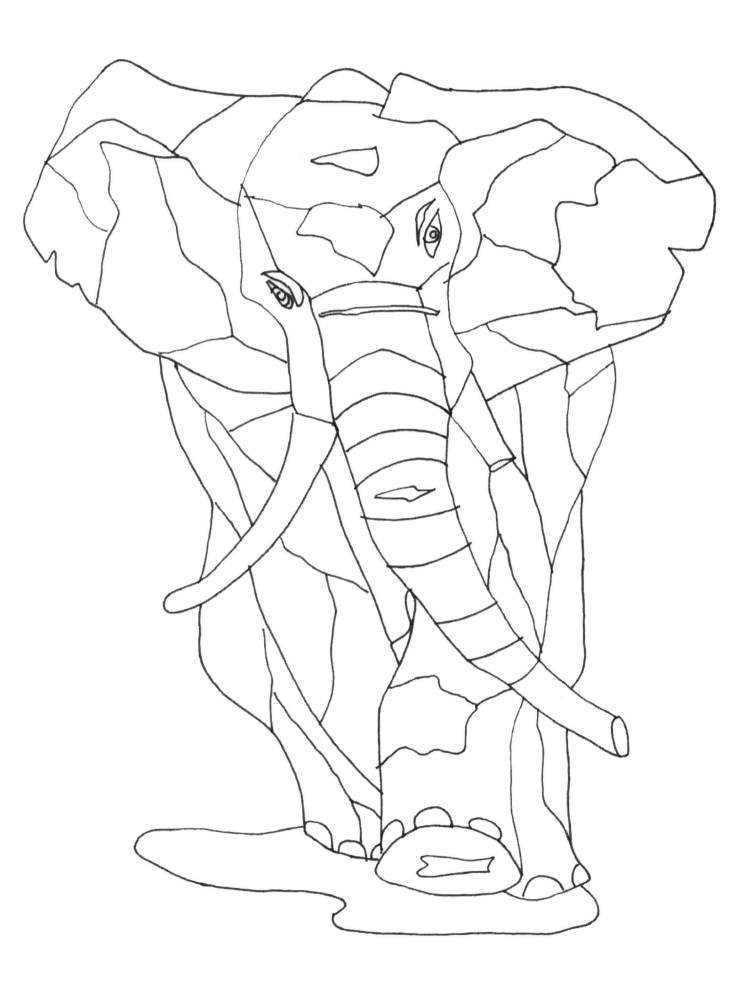

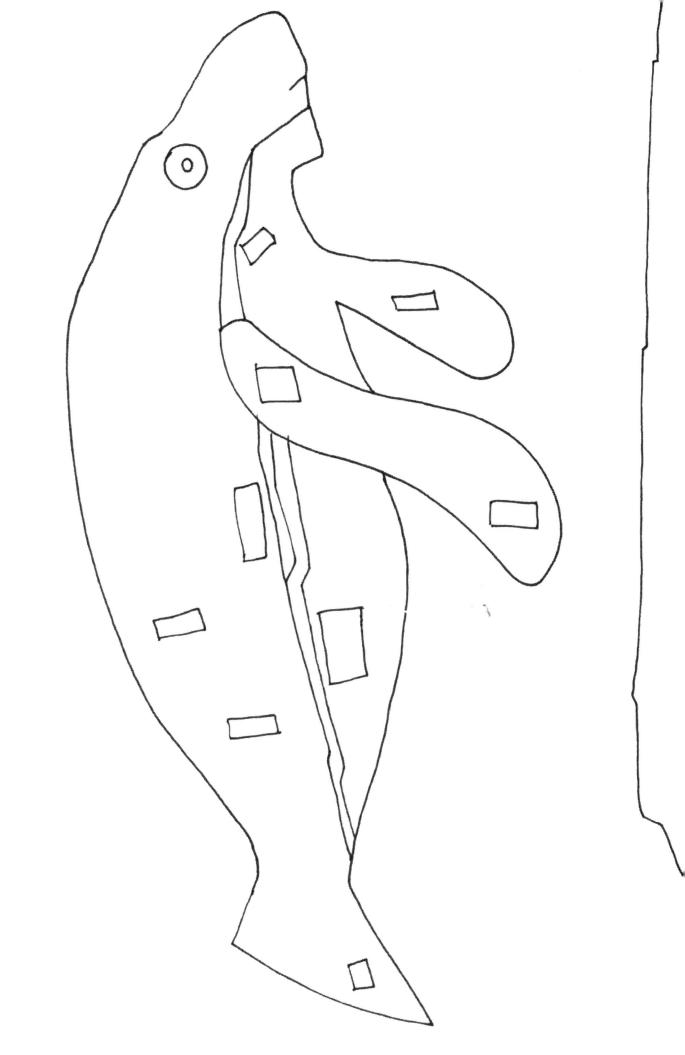

Life!

Animal Farm

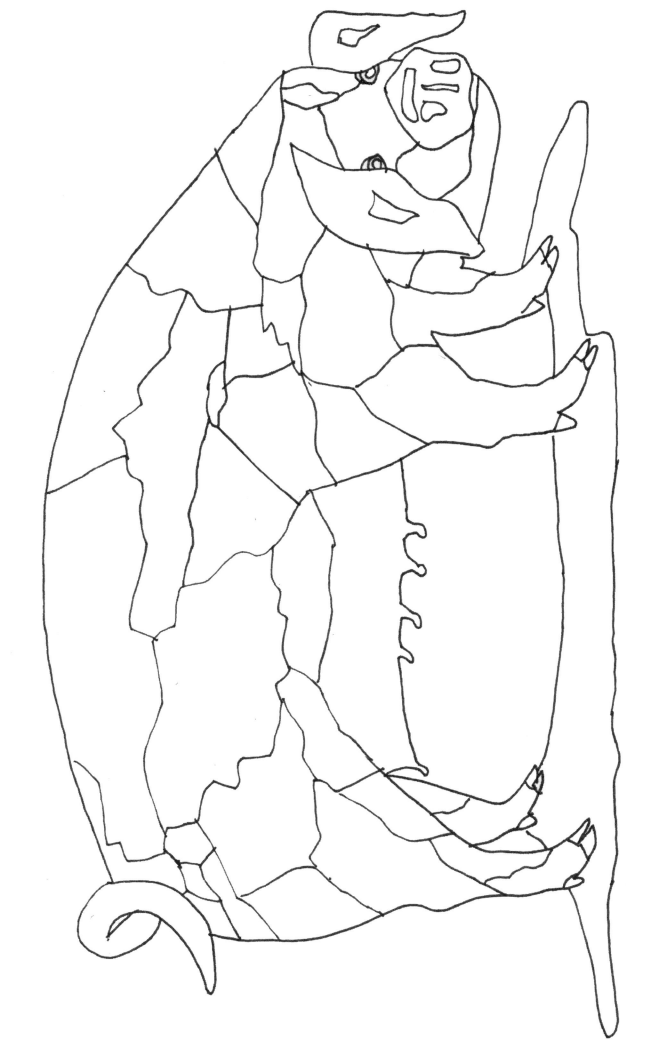

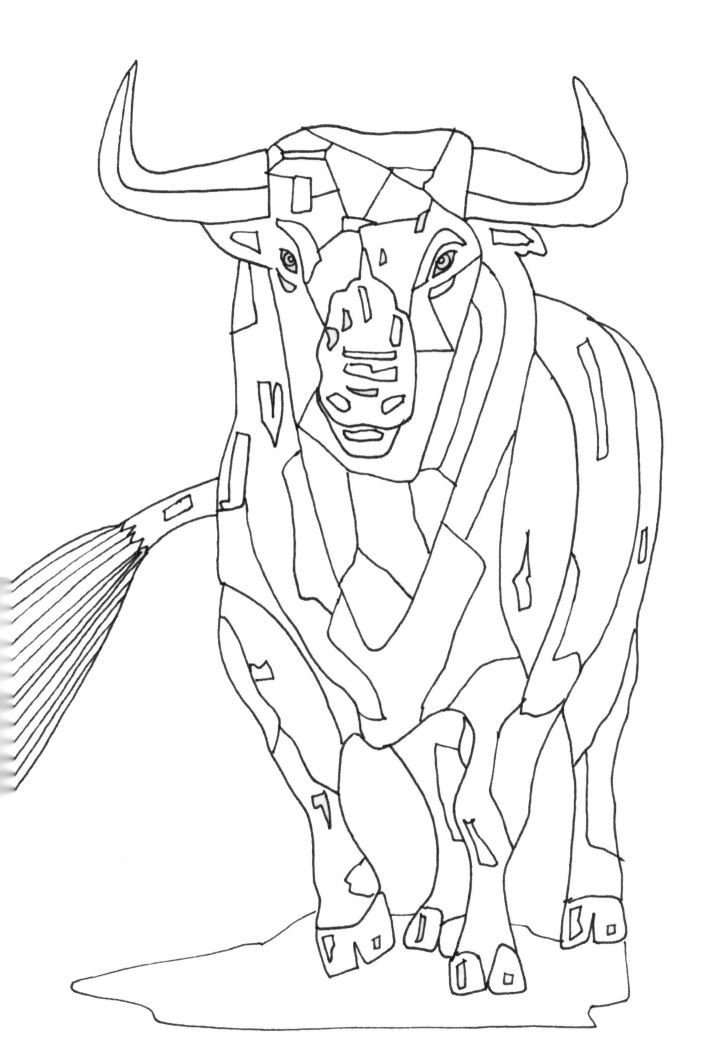

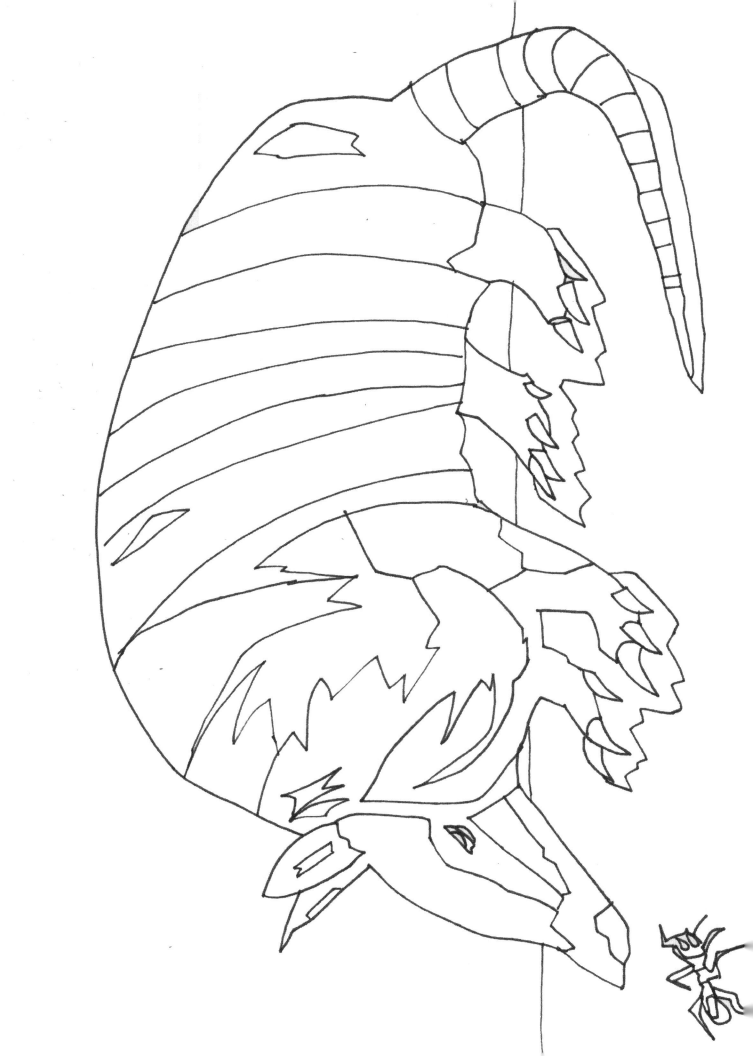

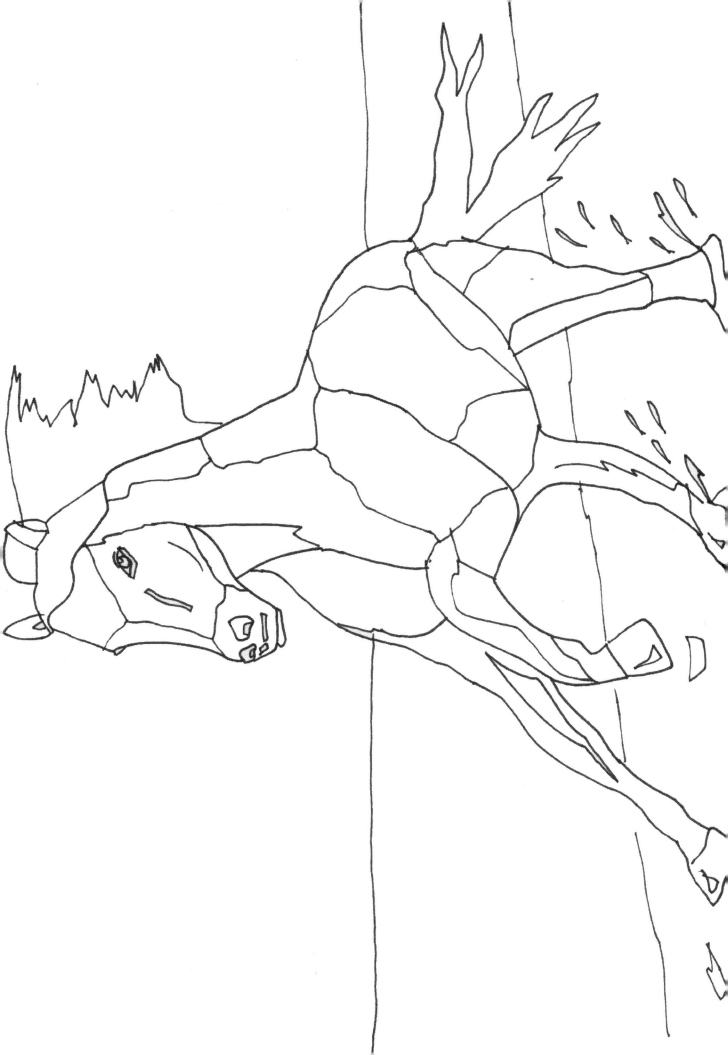

Yellowstone

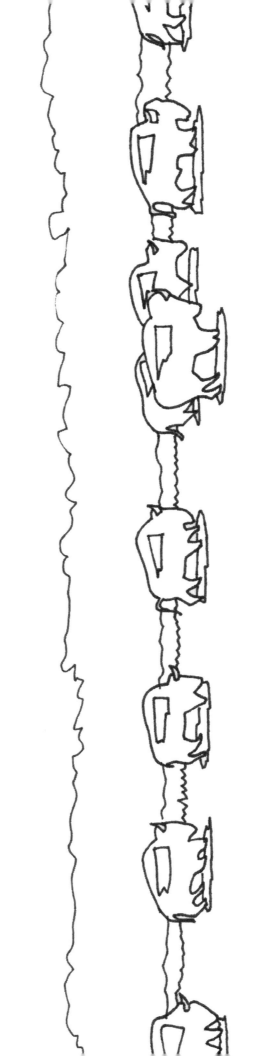

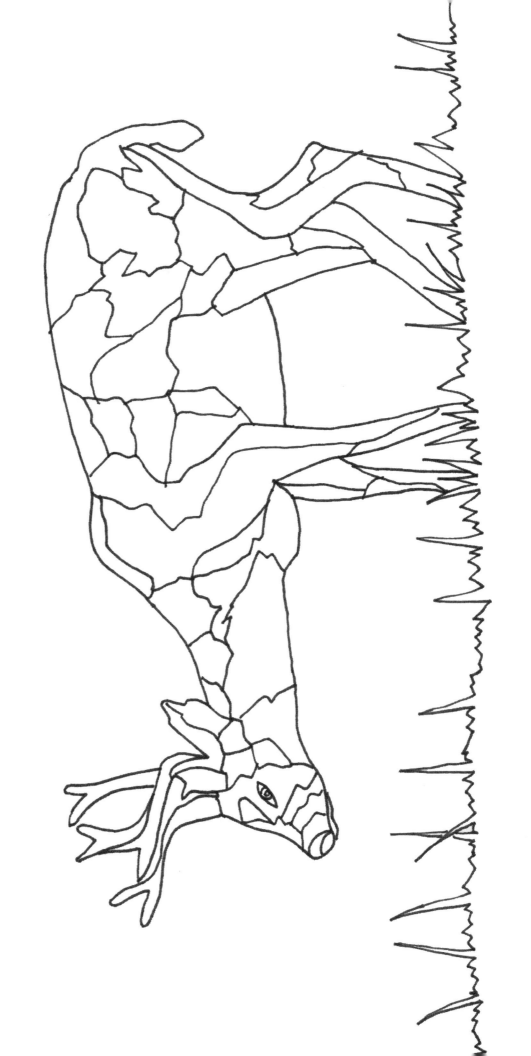

Colorado Wildlife

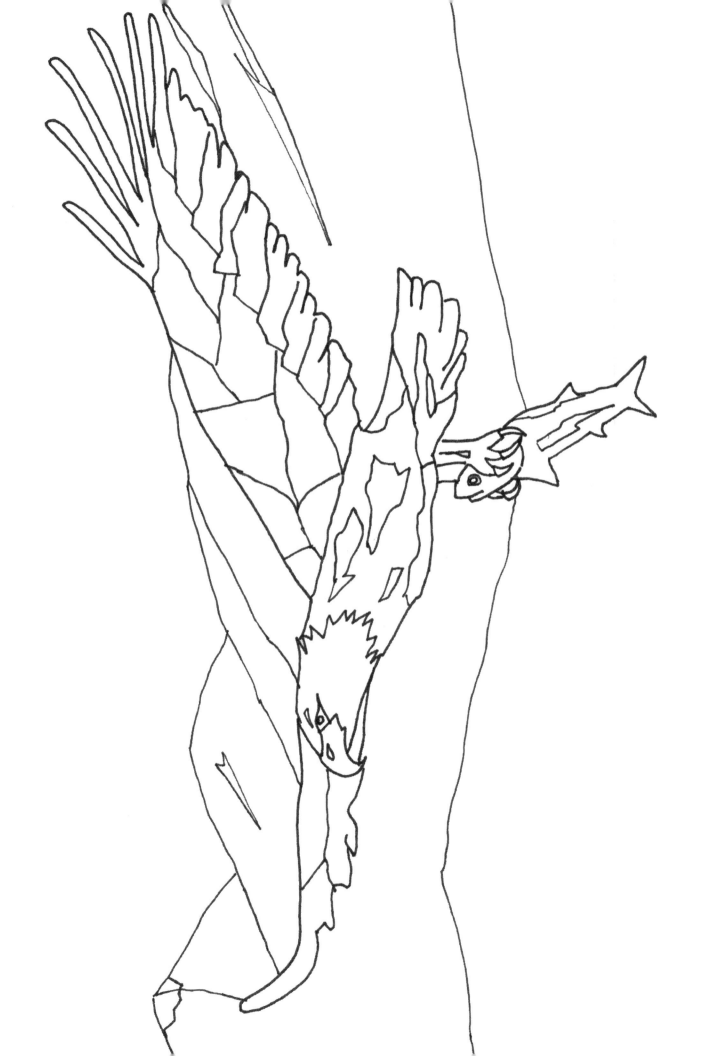

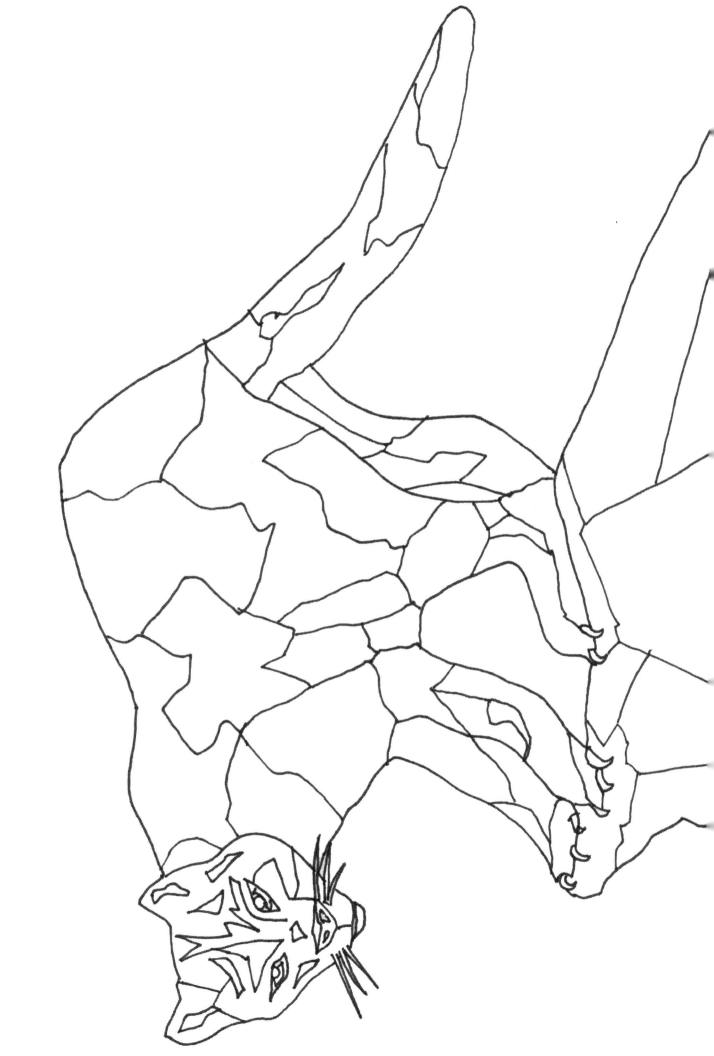

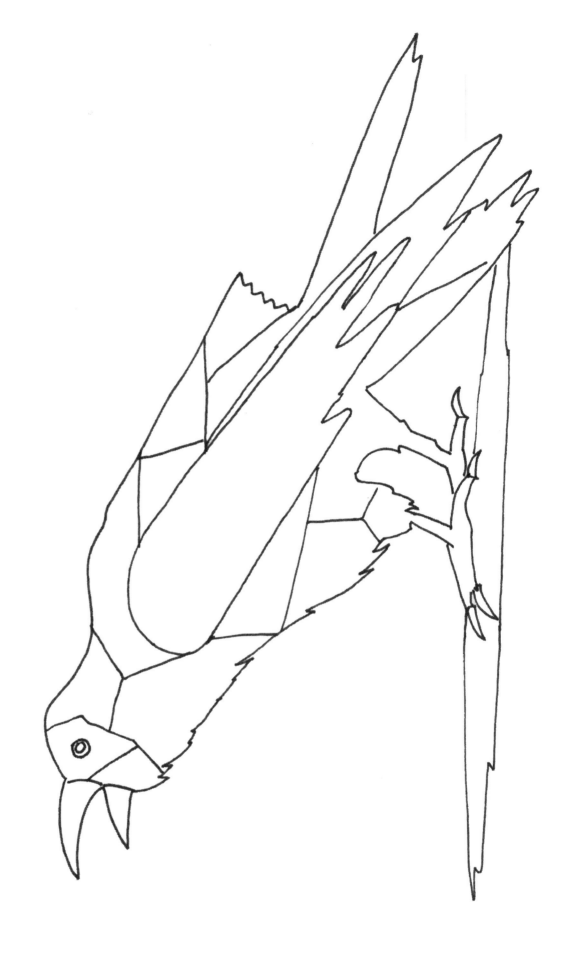

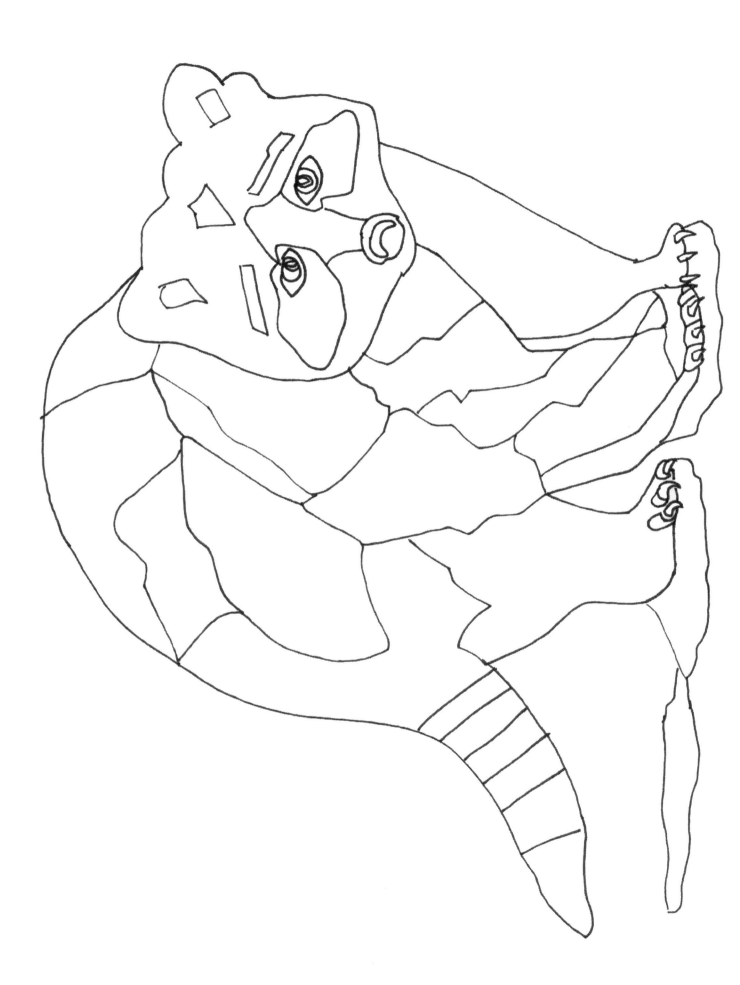

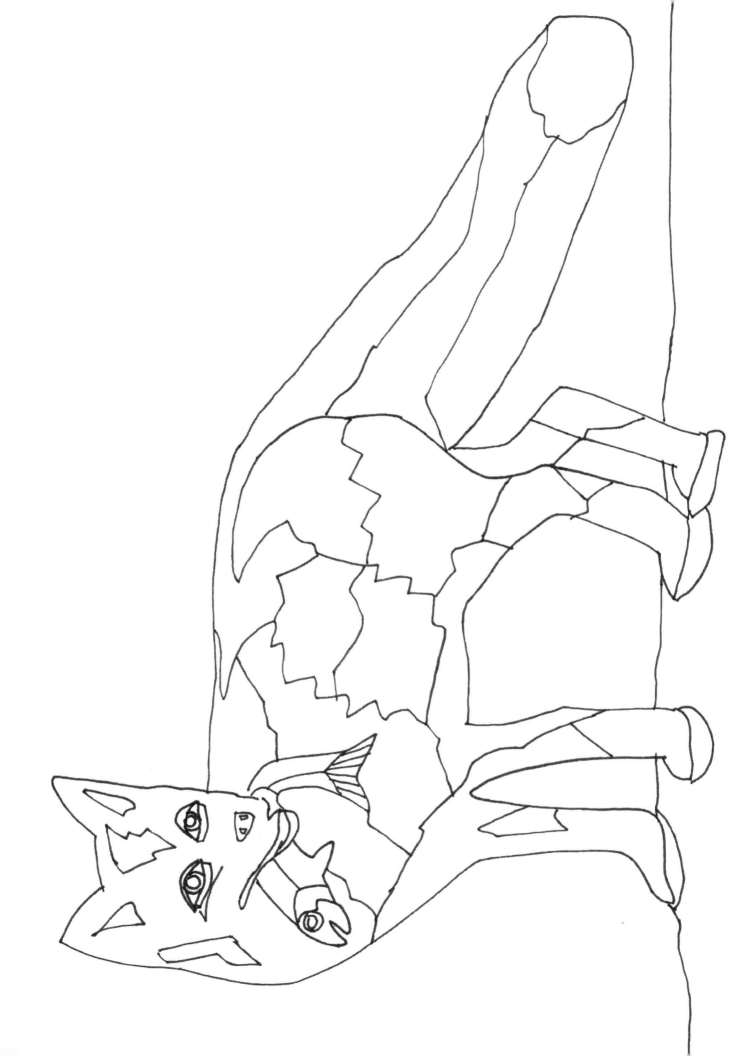

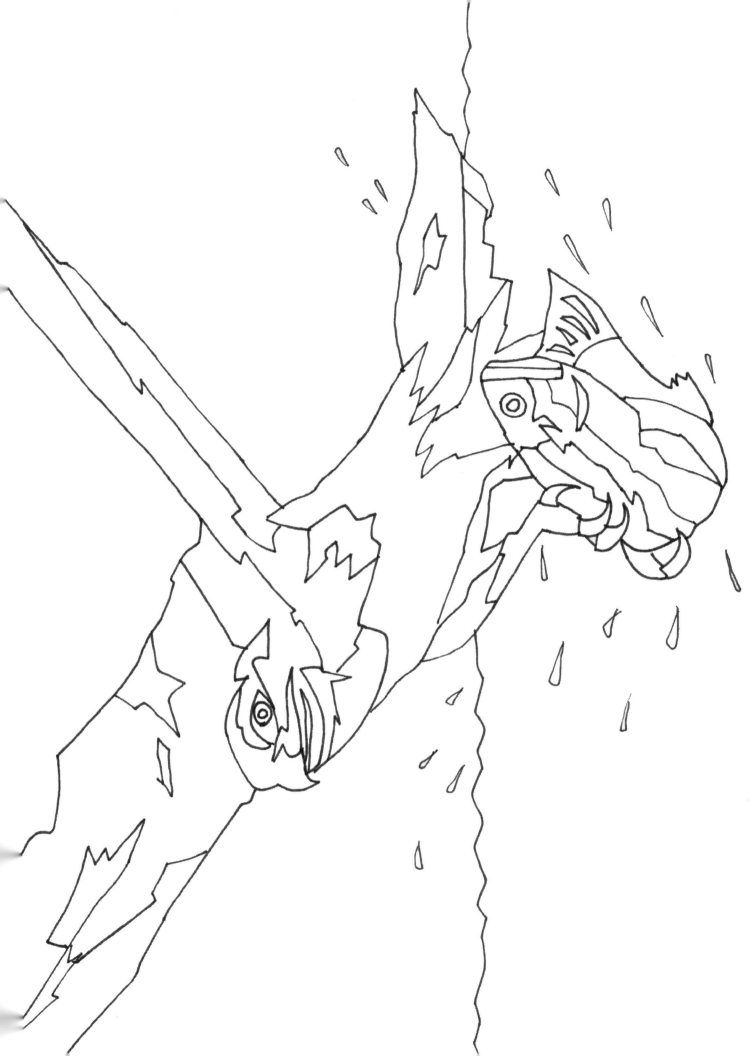

Australia

Antartica

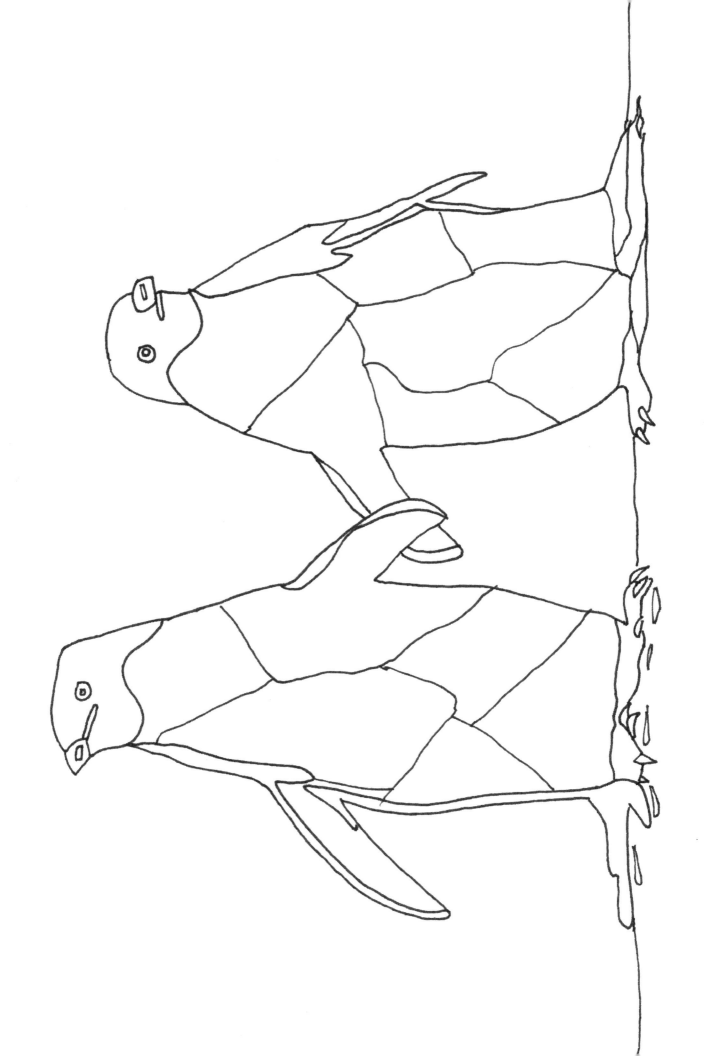

Create your own animal here...
And don´t forget to smile!

Made in the USA
San Bernardino, CA
17 October 2017